Listening
With Your
Heart

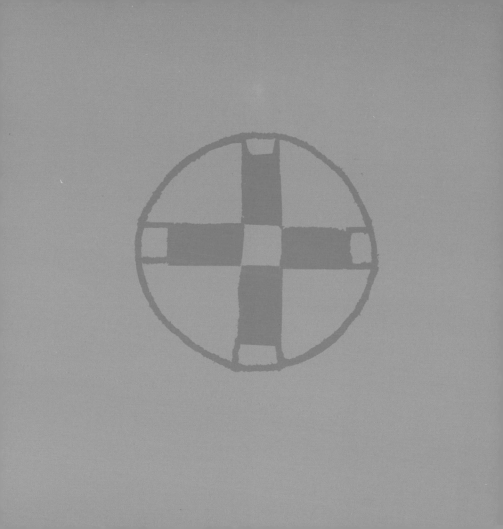

Listening With Your Heart

Lessons from Native America

W. F. Peate, M.D.

Rio Nuevo Publishers
Tucson, Arizona

Never forget the sky, the earth, the wind,
     the rain
And Great Eagle, who brings night and day
     from the four directions.
Never forget the sun, who breathes
     healthful life on the earth.

~*song of the Plains people*

INTRODUCTION

"Dr. Peate, which do you think is best for my husband, alternative or modern medicine?" asked the wife of one of my patients.

My answer was, "Whatever works."

Open a newspaper or turn on a television, and you'll predictably be informed about the latest health innovation. Alternative medicine, holistic health, and spiritual healing are promoted as recent improvements over modern medicine. You might be surprised to discover that all these have been practiced by Native peoples for thousands of years, and that effective healers respect both modern and traditional approaches.

For me, it all began when I was serving as a senior medical student on the Navajo Reservation years ago.

Old Man Hosteen, an elderly Navajo man, lay comatose in the ICU bed like a chocolate mummy swaddled in bandages. His blood pressure was in the stratosphere, and we weren't able to do anything about it. I've found there is something surreal, otherworldly, when you're this close to death. The angels wait for a misstep, an error, or sometimes just an inevitability.

Then a man who smelled like a musty campfire blocked my view—a Navajo healer, I learned later. The nurses hushed me as the man sprinkled cornmeal on the four corners of Hosteen's bed and began a high-pitched chant. I checked Hosteen's blood pressure. It had fallen to normal! Old Man Hosteen later said he was going towards a light when he heard the healer's chant, and that it was those soothing words that brought him back to life.

He was right.

Although I am descended through my mother from the Mohawk and Onondaga Nations of the Iroquois, this was my first experience with Native healing. As a medical student I was being trained to hear hearts with my stethoscope, but I found I was missing a great deal by not listening with *my* heart.

So began a journey. Native healers helped me find not only a bridge between ancient wisdom and modern breakthroughs, but also a pathway to personal fulfillment. Patients were no longer *problems* to listen to, but fellow travelers to listen and grow with. As a physician, I've learned to discern the fears behind the brave face that has just heard the words: "I'm sorry, but you have cancer." As a physician, researcher, teacher, husband, and father, I have grown to be able to hear the rhythm of others' unspoken needs, the tune of acceptance when no more can be done, the powerful beat when healing overcomes sickness, and the melodies of other nations whose diversity is our strength.

Those healers who have generously shared their knowledge and their stories of listening with their hearts will remain anonymous, preserving the traditional privacy of healer and patient. May their methods guide you on your journey to well-being.

W. F. Peate, M.D.

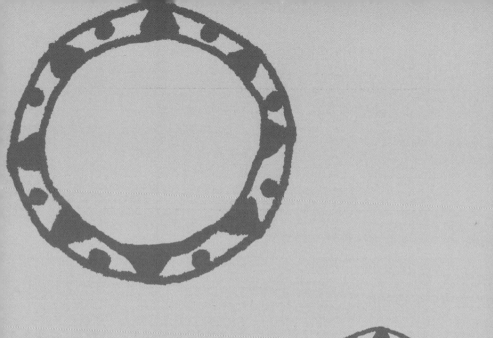

The white man talks about the mind and body and spirit as if they are separate. For us they are one. Our whole life is spiritual, from the time we get up until we go to bed.

~Yakima healer

Breathe in the light of the new day,
    the dawn.
Give thanks for the new day, for those
    around you, for life, for everything.
Then you will become whole again.

~*Navajo healer*

THE POWER
OF FOUR

The number four has a special significance in tribal cultures. The Iroquois built their longhouses oriented to the sacred four directions. Even tribes are sometimes divided into fourths—the traditional Tsimshian of the Pacific Northwest were organized into four clans. And quartets of symbols resonate in Native healing. Four sacred materials are often evident in weavings, sculpture, paintings, and jewelry, and are also essential to many healing practices. Healers compose herbal formulas from four strong medicines and balance them according to individual need.

And four sacred directions are used to help the ill recover.

FOUR SACRED PATHS TO HEALTH

△ NORTH   The spirit runs through the body—spirituality and healing

▷ EAST   The power of relationships—healing as a group activity

◁ WEST   Restoring healing balance—Native healers

▽ SOUTH   The healing life cycle—beginnings, endings, and the next world

△

NORTH: THE HEALING SPIRIT RUNS THROUGH THE BODY

Native healing is a partnership with yourself. When things don't get better, the solution may be inside your own head, within your soul. Native healers believe you have everything you need inside you.

▷

East: The healing power of relationships

Native healing is a partnership with others—family members, community. A Native healer once paraphrased Abraham Lincoln to me: "You can heal some things all of the time," the healer said, "and you can heal all things some of the time, but you can't heal everything all the time alone." Everyone needs a coach, a family, a community.

WEST: RESTORING HEALING
BALANCE—NATIVE HEALERS

Native healing is a partnership between the healer and you. It is just as important to become the right patient as it is to find the right healer or healing method. Native healing requires active participation by the one to be healed.

SOUTH: THE HEALING LIFE CYCLE—FROM BIRTH TO DEATH TO THE NEXT WORLD

Native healing is a partnership for life between healer and patient. It has its beginnings and endings, and although the middle sometimes isn't easy, especially after your initial enthusiasm has faded, there is fulfillment and healing harmony at the end.

THE FOUR NAVAJO PRINCIPAL ELEMENTS

 The Sun that brings warmth

The Earth that gives nourishment

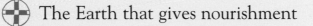 The Wind that brings the rain clouds

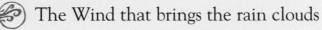 The Rain that gives life-giving moisture

One hopes to live to an old age and to live
a life guided by beauty, the Beauty Way.

~Navajo healer

HEALING WORDS

Hozho (*HO-zo, from Navajo*) A complex Navajo philosophical, religious, and aesthetic concept roughly translated as "beauty." Hozho also means seeking and incorporating aesthetic qualities into life, it means inner peace and harmony, and it means making the most of all that surrounds us. It refers to a positive, beautiful, harmonious, happy environment that must be constantly created by thought and deed. Hozho encourages us to go in beauty and to enjoy the gifts of life and nature and health.

Wak'a *(WAH-kah, from Quechua)* An Inca word meaning sacredness, including the sacred connection between body and spirit, individual and cosmos. Sometimes spelled "huaca," "guaca,"or "juaca" in Spanish, the term also refers to ancient deities, pre-Columbian artifacts, sacred shrines and archaeological sites (particularly ceremonial pyramids or temples), places underground, and hidden treasure.

JOYFUL I JOURNEY

Joyful I journey.
Joyful with life-bringing rain clouds I journey.
Joyful with refreshing rain I journey.
Joyful with growing plants I journey.
Joyful on the pollen trail I journey.
Joyful I journey.

As it was long ago I journey.
Let there be beauty before me.
Let there be beauty behind me.
Let there be beauty below me.
Let there be beauty all around me.
In beauty it is complete.
In beauty it is complete.

~Navajo chant

Spirituality can also ease the burden when healing is not possible. May the story give you strength. May the belief relieve your pain.

~Native American saying

Sialim tago Jiosh E-Tonalic O-Himetha.
O Creator, listen, forgive, and have mercy.
~Tohono O'odham prayer

BOTANICAL HEALING

One in five modern prescription drugs contains an ingredient from a flowering plant. One in five plants has a documented medical use, as Native healers are well aware. In this book you'll find information on traditional uses of maple, curly dock, pine, foxglove, tobacco, soapwort, peppermint, strawberry leaves, saw palmetto, and prickly pear cactus.

(Note: Before beginning any treatment, see your doctor.)

MAPLE (*Acer* SPP.)

Maple syrup was originally produced by the Indians of the St. Lawrence River and Great Lakes regions. It is created from the sweet watery sap of the sugar maple (*Acer saccharum*) and the black maple (*Acer niger*) that is concentrated through evaporation. Native peoples would lightly sweeten water with maple syrup to soothe an irritable baby. (Don't substitute honey in children under one year of age because of bacterial concerns.) Maple leaves on the forehead, chest, or wrists offer cooling relief, too.

NOT ALONE

We are not alone.
The spirits of those gone before guide our
steps, our traditions, our beliefs.
We are not alone.
The care of those around us leads us to
healing and wholeness and comfort.
We are not alone.

~Mohawk/Onondaga healer

Every action should be taken with thoughts of its effects on children seven generations from now.

~Cherokee saying

CURLY DOCK (*Ramex crispus*)

Sometimes modernity creates disease. Traditionally, Native peoples and others, including our ancestors, cooked in iron utensils whose use added essential iron to their diets and helped prevent anemia. Modern salespeople persuaded them to buy shiny aluminum pans, and iron-deficiency anemia started to rise. Fortunately, many edible plants are iron-rich, such as curly dock or *Ramex crispus*.

To prepare curly dock greens, pick the younger leaves at the top, boil until the leaves are limp, and serve. Some people add vinegar. Avoid plants by a roadside that might have been exposed to herbicide, automobile fuels, oils, or lubricants.

The wind may blow, but it will never move the mountain, until it brings life-giving rain that melts the earth away.

~Navajo healer

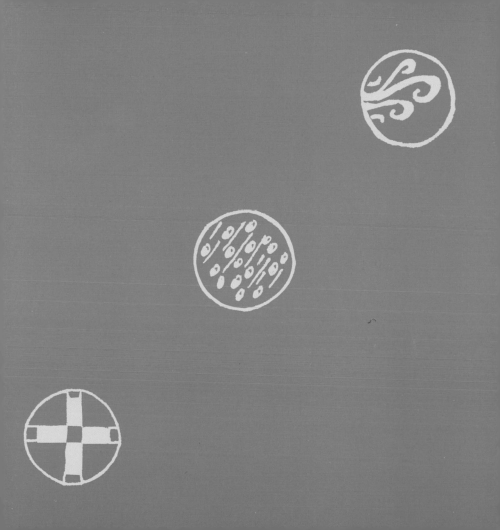

 Botanical Healing

PINE (*Pinus* SPP.)

The great Iroquois leader Hiawatha (c. 1450) is one of those rare figures in human history who chose an unexpected path to healing: peace. Instead of plotting destruction, he planned and skillfully crafted an enduring compact between his tribe and five others, a treaty that ended war and ensured regional harmony for the benefit of all. Weapons were buried at the base of a prominent white pine tree, and pine needles from that species (*Pinus stobus*) have been used by Native healers ever since.

White-pine needles are actually a good source of vitamin C and when chewed also serve as a mouth freshener. If brewed, they make a refreshing tea or body wash.

The Iroquois used other plant products for their medicinal properties, especially meadow rue and the bark of trees such as the wild cherry and willow (which contains salicin, a chemical related to aspirin). "Adirondack" is an Iroquois term for "bark-eater."

THREE GIFTS
OF HEALERS

EMPOWERMENT

Medicine people know prayers for empowerment.
They can reach into the innermost person and enhance
that person's innate abilities, hopes, and dreams.

PREVENTION

Our sleep-dreams can foretell the future. Therefore
future harms can be prevented.

HUMOR

Laughter is a proven stress reliever, and Native healers employ it generously.

~Navajo healer

You Westerners miss half of life—your dreams.
Use them to your will.

Andean healer

Whatever you need to know, dreams can reveal.

~Andean healer

Botanical Healing

FOXGLOVE *(Digitalis purpurea)*

Foxglove (and its derivative, digitalis) is a powerful heart botanical that has been used by many cultures—including mainstream Western medicine—for thousands of years for conditions such as heart failure and the irregular heart rhythm known as atrial fibrillation (the elder George Bush suffered from this condition). Overdosage was somewhat easier to monitor with the traditional botanical than it is with purified digitalis. And dosage is critical: Recently, some women who used a mixture of herbs, including foxglove, for "internal cleansing" suffered from digitalis toxicity (such as vision problems, nausea, and heart disturbances). Never use foxglove or digitalis unless prescribed by a licensed medical professional.

I turn the corner with the patient
and then we are in the light.

~Yakima healer

To Native healers, "light" is a vision of well-being where broken hearts and bodies are healed, and where many times the true cause of an illness is found. Once found, it is more easily remedied.

~*Yakima healer*

Light is a gift given in the spirit. There is no money that can buy it—you just go through it from two years old 'til the day you decide to die. When medicine men are ready to go, they go. They aren't sick—they just decide they've done what they wanted to do.

~Yakima healer

TOBACCO (*Nicotiana* SPP.)

Many Native healers use tobacco in ceremonies. You might ask: Isn't that contrary to healthy living? Some physicians have observed that the use of limited amounts of tobacco for ceremonial purposes, not to feed an addiction, is not harmful. In fact, if you want to limit the use of a substance, use it for religious purposes. For this reason Indians have a lower rate of tobacco use than other groups, just as Jews who use alcohol for weekly Sabbath ceremonies have lower rates of alcoholism than the rest of the population.

The tribe or family works because when one
member is down, the others can pick him or her up.
What we have, including our wealth, is to be shared.

~Onondaga elder

Ceremonies are so a person may speak from the heart and know his thoughts are respected. I have a bright light I enter when I do a healing ceremony. In the scientific world you go from A to B. When I perform a ceremony the light goes up and down, sideways and all around.

~Yakima healer

Once you go into a ceremony, you go into the light, around the curve, and you bring your patients back from another world where they are already dead, from lack of spirituality.

~*Yakima healer*

SOAPWORT *(Saponaria officinalis)*

Soapwort Shampoo

Take the soapwort (or bouncing bet) plant, roots and all, and cover and soak in water for half an hour. (In the western United States, you can substitute yucca roots.) Puree and strain through cheesecloth or a coffee filter. Warm it and work into your hair. Refrigerate the unused portion, and it will last three to four weeks.

We are made up of prayers. With prayer we listen to what is really important inside of us and all around us—the Beauty Way.

~Navajo healer

The Beauty Way

To walk in beauty is to live a life of inner tranquility and fulfillment. The Beauty Way enables you to tap into the good that is all around you, to peel back your layers of lost hopes, fears, and drudgery, and live your dreams again. The healer or *hataalii* teaches you to call on the power of the good forces all around us, not just in the sweat lodge, but anywhere, anytime.

~Navajo healer

NINE TECHNIQUES TO RESTORE ONE TO THE BEAUTY WAY

First

Dedicate your sleep to gain knowledge. Dreams can reveal a great deal about what troubles you.

Second

Close your eyes and you see better and hear better.

Third

Ceremonies can remove obstructions. And ceremonies do not have to be elaborate, just something as simple as taking time each morning to feel the dawn.

Fourth

Rise before sunrise and bathe in the coolness. It will help wash badness away, and you'll be able to handle any situation.

Fifth

Smile about the problems you receive; they build muscle. Serendipity is around every corner and life detour.

Sixth

What's important is not what happened, but to rebuild.

Seventh

Life is great, life is good, especially when you share it with someone.

Eighth

Teach all the time, and learn all the time.

Ninth

The final technique to restore one to the Beauty Way is prayer. When you pray long enough you will find shortcuts to the best path to take.

~Navajo healer

Breathe in the dawn four times.
Breathe out a prayer to yourself,
To the dawn, the universe.
It is holy, all holy once more.

~Navajo prayer

A ceremony for persons with an illness calms them, they feel less pain, their symptoms settle down. Their minds go into the light, into another place. If they can do this, they feel better.

~*Native healer*

PEPPERMINT (*Mentha* SPP.)
AND STRAWBERRY (*Fragaria* SPP.)

Peppermint leaves make a soothing tea. If mixed with strawberry leaves, the combination aids digestion.

Peppermint-Strawberry Tea

Combine:

8 fresh peppermint leaves

4 fresh strawberry leaves

2 cups water

Crush leaves, place in teapot. Add boiling water and cover for 10 minutes. Strain and serve.

CEREMONY

America claims it is a land that left
     ceremony behind.
No kings are crowned here on the backs
     of peasants,
And tradition is discarded as the dead
     ceremony of the living.
But we traditionalists know
Our ceremonies are our strength that
     sustains us.
The birthing of a new child,
The wedding of husband and wife,

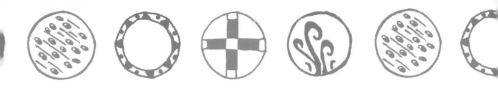

The teaching of the wise elder,
The healing of those ill in body and mind.

These and more are our ceremonies.
They were our strength when everything
    was taken away,

They will renew us in hard times ahead.
They make us strong.
They are our strength.

~Cherokee healer

The sweat lodge is a spiritual experience that brings us into harmony and balance with the world. It brings a positive out of a negative. Fire is quenched by rain. The pain of childbirth is softened by the birth of a new life.

~Navajo healer

When we help others, we help ourselves. It's not good to get too focused on your own problems, especially when others need more than you.

~Oneida saying

SAW PALMETTO (*Serenoa serrulata*)

As adult males age, their prostate glands enlarge, urination becomes more frequent and less forceful, and nightly trips to the toilet become more common. To treat enlarged prostate symptoms, Southern tribes used saw palmetto berries with some success.

Note: See your doctor if you have symptoms.

Usual dose: Take 200 mg two times a day.

Usually 3–4 weeks are required to see effects.

THE POLLEN PATHWAY

If gold is your hunger,
Let the yellow of honey sweeten your day,
Let the yellow of the sun grow the plants
    in your fields,
Let the amber of the corn feed your children,
Let the gold of the sunset warm your soul.
Follow the gold of the pollen way
And you will be happy with all the riches that
    you have.

~Native healer

PRICKLY PEAR (*Opuntia* SPP.)

Tohono O'odham cooks prepare traditional foods such as prickly-pear cactus pads or *nopales*, called *nopalitos* when small and edible, which contain substances (mucopolysaccharides) that partially neutralize the effects of diabetes. The fruit of this cactus (along with the fruit of other varieties of *Opuntia*) is also edible.

Note: See your doctor if you have or believe you have diabetes.

Nopalitos (Cactus Pads)

Preparation: Use tongs to collect the young, tender pads. (Occasionally they may be purchased raw in vegetable markets.) Boil for 15 minutes. Place on cutting board, hold down with a fork, and scrape off stickers with a knife. Cut off base of pad and ⅛ inch around the pad's edge.

Nopalito Salad

2 prepared pads (see previous page)
2 cups shredded carrots
1 cup shredded apple
¼ cup milk
¼ cup chopped dates (optional)

Cut prickly-pear pad into strips ¼ inch wide and dry in a flat pan in the sun for three hours, or overnight, until strips are chewy. Chop into small pieces. In a bowl, combine all ingredients.

Note: Canned or frozen nopalitos are sometimes available from specialty food suppliers.

Prickly Pear Fruit Strips

Pick the prickly-pear fruit with tongs, place them in a large plastic container, rinse, and freeze them. Then allow them to defrost. Press them with a potato masher and then pour the "purple mess" through a fine-mesh colander. Mix 4 cups of prickly-pear juice with 4 teaspoons of honey and 6 ounces of grape juice or other fruit concentrate. Spread on a cookie sheet covered with plastic wrap. Dry in an oven at the lowest setting; this can take all day. After the fruit leather is dry, peel the plastic off, roll up in strips, and enjoy.

The heavens may send driving snow and bitter ice, but nature is in harmony. To find harmony man must also travel the path through storms and turmoil. And so the magic of the great peace came to the five nations, and the warmth of their stronger sun gave healing light.

~Iroquois saying

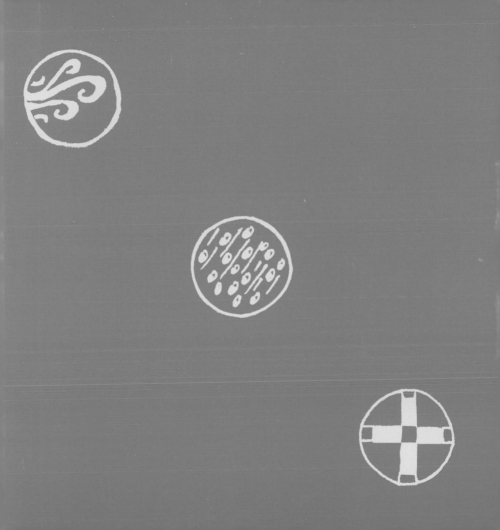

NOT FOREVER

Does one really live upon the earth?
Not forever on the earth, only for a short
    time here.
Even jade shatters
Even gold breaks
Even quetzal plumes tear
Not forever on the earth, only a short
    time here.

~Nahuatl (Aztec) poem

THE BEYOND

Native healers see "the beyond," and what we call
death, as a transition to the next world.

THE TAKING UP

One Native healer described the "taking up" of the dead by departed family members.

"Suddenly the light changes over the dead person," he said. "A whirling mass of roundish lights appears, leaving a dark trail behind it, all in an area of four to five feet in diameter, unlike anything you've ever seen before. It is not like what you see when electrical lights in the room change, flicker, or dim."

He went on: "The entire room fills with something— energy. At the same time 'something' concentrates near the head of the dead person.

"Then," he said, "you feel that the 'somethings' within this whirling mass of lights have personality. They might be ticked off, angry—maybe at me or the family or the situation of death delayed unnecessarily by futile medical intervention? The source of this feeling has a name, sometimes of a departed relative. Others are there, perhaps many."

He paused, and then he continued: "They gather up something from the dead person, their soul, spirit, consciousness…a light seems to remove itself from the dead person, and then everything appears to vanish from the room."

Along with this movement, according to the healer, comes a sound of energy and a fluttering like feathers. Was this why the ancients believed angels had wings? But the healer said it sounded more like a mechanical noise, which ancient people may never have heard. In our time, power sounds are common.

"The light changes over the dead, becomes less illuminated," the healer went on, "and the dead one is finally and fully gone."

THE CEMETERY

"This one is ready to speak," said the Tohono O'odham healer, walking among the graves of his people. He touched his long, gnarled walking stick, which looked like a thin dark muscled arm, against another grave. "This one isn't ready."

BLESSING

I am whole, I am healthy, I am not the disease,
I am part of the eternal greatness.
May this story give you strength. You have
    everything you need.
Look North: the spirit runs through the body.
Look East and feel the power of the Sun,
    our family, our people.
Look West and hold on to a healing guide.
Look South and make harmony with your life.

~Native healer

A NATIVE HEALER'S PRESCRIPTION FOR HEALTH

R_x: Take small miracles daily.

• • • • •

For a second, let it stop: the rush, the deadline, the self-imposed slavery of "must do."

• • • • •

For a moment, close your eyes in the darkness and see the dancing stars behind your eyelids.

For a minute, see a magnificent flower in your mind. Add the sound of a soothing waterfall and then the smell of cool mint.

· · · · ·

For a time, feel each breath.

With each breath out, imagine releasing a pain, an ache, a worry.

With each breath in, absorb a sense of comfort, a kind word, a selfless act, a memory of the best thing this year.

FOR A LIFE, REMEMBER:

North... In the spring the corn tassel blossoms
with new life.

East... In the summer the flower partners with the bee
to fertilize and yield fruit.

West... In the fall the people harvest the fruit
to sustain life.

South... In the winter the mountains grow white
beards, and the people store food and seed to begin again,
and again, and again.

Find peace, health, wholeness, connection,
and completion in the small miracles.

~Mohawk/Onondaga healer

To my loving wife, Lynn.
Thank you for two decades of sharing dreams,
bedtime stories, and healing secrets.

Rio Nuevo Publishers
An imprint of Treasure Chest Books
P.O. Box 5250, Tucson, Arizona 85703-0250
(520) 623-9558
www.rionuevo.com

Design: Dawn DeVries Sokol

ISBN 1-887896-52-X
Printed in Korea
19 18 17 16 15 14 13 12

• • • • • • • • • • • • • • • •

Descended from the Mohawk and Onondaga Nations of the Iroquois, Dr. W. F. Peate
received his medical education at Dartmouth and Harvard. He has also lived and
worked with Native peoples and healers in Africa, Latin America, and the reservations
and barrios of the United States. He practices and teaches medicine and public health
at the University of Arizona in Tucson and in Dr. Andrew Weil's Integrative Medicine
Program. He is also the author of *Native Healing: Four Sacred Paths to Health* (Rio
Nuevo Publishers, 2002).